I'LL HOLD
YOU IN
HEAVEN

JACK HAYFORD

Chosen

a division of Baker Publishing Group
Minneapolis, Minnesota

© 1986, 1990, 2003 by Jack W. Hayford

Published by Chosen Books
11400 Hampshire Avenue South
Bloomington, Minnesota 55438
www.chosenbooks.com

Chosen Books is a division of
Baker Publishing Group, Grand Rapids, Michigan

Chosen Books edition published 2015
ISBN 978-0-8007-9661-7

This revised and updated edition previously published by Regal Books.
The essential substance of this book first published in the Living
Way Paperback *Early Flight,* © 1986.

Printed in the United States of America

Library of Congress Catalog Number: 2014956819

21   7

CONTENTS

INTRODUCTION

*The Spirit of the LORD is upon Me, because He has . . . sent
Me to heal the brokenhearted.*

LUKE 4:18

As a pastor—a shepherd of souls—I find myself, time and time again, meeting people who have suffered the death of a baby, either before or shortly after birth. If you have experienced the great crisis to which I refer, it's quite possible that you are searching for something—anything—powerful enough to calm the questions that may rage inside your heart.

You may be among the great number of women and men who have planned, prepared and prayed for a child, but the baby was still-born—dead on arrival. Perhaps you are one of the thousands of parents whose newborn babies lived so short a life as to have hardly truly arrived—babies who died a few hours, days or weeks after birth. Together, parents of the still-born and of the newly born who die form a distinct group of people who had a baby they never got to keep.

Or maybe you are the parent of a child lost to abortion. If so, you may be like so many others I meet who are suffering greatly in the aftermath of the procedure that proponents hail as prompt and painless. Untold numbers of women and men are stumbling through the emotional carnage following an abortion—some believing their decision was wrong; others racked with uncertainty. The pain runs deep.

Finally, you may belong to a third group of the disappointed: the hosts of women who longed for a child, but two or three—four or maybe five—months into their pregnancy something went awry and they miscarried.

If you have experienced the wrenching loss of a child in the womb or during the weeks and months following birth, you are hardly alone. The parents of the stillborn or the newly born who die, the miscarrying mother and the maternal victim of abortion are all parents of children who were designed for a lifetime of purpose but whose lives were cut short.

In the Creator's finest plan, these children were not intended for the disease, death or destruction that took their lives. Yet they died. Like a rescheduled airplane suddenly departing ahead of time, these children took an "early flight." Before we could ever know them—their possibilities, their presence and their purpose— they were gone. Whether their hastened departure was forced through accident, neglect or abuse of the fetus, disease, deformity or simple malfunction, suddenly they departed.

For those who remain at the airport of the present, there can be tears, pain, bitterness and questions—but I assure you that there is also hope.

In recent years, as I encountered increasing numbers of hurting people whose parenthood had been cut short, I began to search God's Word to seek a case for *hope*. I wanted to find truth that could heal and give comfort in the midst of the pain following the amputation of a life from its potential; thus, this book.

In the following chapters you will find scripturally based answers to many of the questions you may have found yourself asking: *At the time of my miscarriage or abortion, did my baby have a soul? What about the stillborn child or the baby who dies shortly after birth? Is he or she in heaven? If so, what is he or she—this child who never developed character or personality beyond the womb—like? Will I ever see my child again? And how will I recognize my child when we finally meet in heaven?*

The purpose of this book is to offer a path to hope and healing—not through happy talk or platitudes, but through the solid footing of the holy truth of God's Word. The biblical foundation for hope and comfort is strong; the Scriptures indeed offer a way out of the depths of grief.

If you have experienced the loss of a child through the tragedy of abortion, God's Word offers you something more: forgiveness and healing for the series of choices that led you into the abortionist's chamber. Abortion is not only a tough topic but a delicate one. And it's a tragedy. But my object in these pages is not to elaborate that tragedy or underscore the facts of human failure. Rather, I seek to offer comfort and direction for the future.

There was a time when I was not unlike many Christians who wrestle against bitterness, self-righteousness and even condemnation toward the parents of aborted children. I was not only angry that lives were being taken, but I also felt superior. And that was the hateful blindness I had to deal with—the cocksureness of my self-righteous opinion.

In that state, I couldn't even begin to gain perspective on the fear, pain, hurt, agony and embarrassment of so many who needed something else from me. Society has so liberalized abortion that the uninformed and uncounseled readily give in until, in the aftermath of the experience, the living victims bend beneath another burden—the burden of questions such as, What have I done? Who might the child have become? Was I right? Wrong? Can I ever forget? What would have happened if I hadn't . . . ?

Having met increasing numbers of women and men who ache over the ramifications of their right to choose has not changed my conviction about the wrongness of abortion, but it has cured my soul of the wrongness of my superficial point of view. I now see a place where life, light and love are desperately needed—a place in our world where truth not only can shine like a beacon light discerning good and evil but where that same truth can also shed the light of healing, warmth and hopefulness. If you are, indeed, one of the many adult victims of abortion, then read on. You are on the verge of discovering forgiveness, healing and hope.

It is to any parent who remembers—with tears, pain, bitterness or questions—a stillborn, miscarried, aborted or early-death child that I dedicate these moments in God's Word. And for those among us who have never known such pain, failure or grief, my hope is that an enlargement of heart may occur. May God's Spirit, through speaking His Word, create a new space within *all* of us and make a place where we can host with understanding and compassion all those we know or will meet who have been left with aching hearts and empty arms following a little one's early flight from this life.

So now, come with me to the fountain of truth—to God's Word—where eternal wisdom, reconciling righteousness and healing hope abound. Let's find out what we can about God's answers to one of the most wrenching traumas in our present society: the pain following the too-early death of an infant.

I'LL HOLD
YOU IN
HEAVEN

CHAPTER 1

THE GIFT OF LIVES

*And the LORD God formed man of the dust of
the ground, and breathed into his nostrils the breath of life;
and man became a living being.*

GENESIS 2:7

The foundation of hope for any human dilemma or, in fact, for any human disobedience will always be drawn from God's Word—not from human reasoning or happy-talk philosophizing. The answer to your deepest pain or most grievous heart cry lies in Scripture. What then, should be your first question?

Perhaps the best place to begin is with the simple query: *Was my unborn child, in the fullest sense of the meaning, actually a human being?* That question must be settled with confidence and personal certainty. God's answer gives rise to an amazing basis for hope—an expectancy never before anticipated as possible. So let's discover what the Creator Himself has to say on the subject.

Our first objective is to establish a biblical basis for the prenatal existence of the human soul. Is a person a person before he or she is born?

Here is the crux of the matter, for if we are only dealing with chemistry or tissue in examining the nature of the fetus or the stillborn, there is little at stake. But in most of us, an inner monitor signals that there is something more involved here than mere chemical combinations or complex structures of tissues. Could it be that God has given a conclusive and confirming witness in

His Word that the life of an embryo is eternal?

Without surrendering to either mystery or superstition, we can say yes! The life of the child in the womb *is* eternal. But please understand: This is a statement based on far more than religious opinion, occult dogma or human imagination.

The religionist may trumpet the *reality* of and, therefore, the sanctity of life in the womb. But so often these assertions lead to the leveling of accusations. Too easily the focus falls solely on the sin of life's sanctity having been violated, and the hearer rebels. Even if the call to protect life is worthy, it is a false victory to suppose that proclamation is more important than the good news of God's grace, love and healing forgiveness. Life is sacred, to be sure. But many need to see sacred truth that extends beyond that fact—truth that offers other facts after human blindness may have overlooked the first fact of life's sanctity.

On another front, the reincarnationist proposes that all human life is merely the recycling of personalities in new bodies, with the hope of continually improving one's lot in life with each recycling experience. But whatever the wish, hope or pretended logic of such a proposition, honesty requires that we immediately dispense with those notions. God's Word abolishes the phantom philosophies of reincarnation. According to the final revelation of the Bible, life is a one-time proposition for each of us as far as this world is concerned. Life is an appointment that (1) has God's divine purpose, and (2) requires our account-ability: It is appointed unto man to live and die but once—after this comes his evaluation before God.[1]

Contrary to the confused ideas of a few sincere souls, Jesus' words "You must be born again"[2] do not have anything whatsoever to do with another birth beyond this lifetime. Being born again is clearly explained by Jesus Himself. He clarified new birth as an internal renewal, and He specified our need to experience it in *this* lifetime by welcoming Him into our life as Savior and Lord.[3]

Another realm of error distills from the poet-ic notion that while a baby is not a recycled per-sonality having lived life before, each baby had existence prior to the womb. This scenario some-how envisions God as a heavenly Father doling out angel spirits across the earth, installing them in baby bodies either before or at birth. This unscriptural and insensitive idea is at the root of the frequently parroted statement, so sincerely spoken at the funerals of young children, that God somehow knew better and that He took back the life He had earlier given from heaven.

However well intended the thought, God didn't and doesn't take babies because He needs them in heaven. The pain and problem of death exist on this planet because humanity has broken its trust with the treasure of life. And the Bible doesn't say anything at all about God making independent decisions about the placement of each life into each body. Let's see what the Bible does say.

When God Breathes

Genesis 2 elaborates what chapter 1 introduces: God, having created man, told him to be fruitful and multiply. The Word of God then relates how man's possibilities and capabilities for this multiplying were given by his Creator. They are summarized in these words:

> And the LORD God formed man of the dust of the ground, and breathed into his nostrils the breath of life; and man became a living being.[4]

Literally, the Hebrew text reads that God, in creating the father and mother of the race, placed *in them* the capacity to beget life: He breathed into them the breath of *chayeem*—that is, "lives." Notice closely the use of the plural of the word for "life." God gave mankind the gift of *lives*. The concept transcends the obvious Creator-gift of life for each one to *experience* and reaches further to the gift of *lives* placed within each one's capacity to *beget*.

> *We have been given the awesome ability to reproduce eternal* souls *as well as physical* bodies.

First, this ability has been placed at man's discretion. Each time the conception of a child occurs, God does *not* have to take separate action to infuse the fertilized ovum with life. Life is simply *inherently present*—instantly, spontaneously, *always there*—because God delegated "lives" to man for propagation. The awesome ability to reproduce eternal *souls* as well as physical *bodies* has been given to mankind.

Second, until that union of sperm and egg occurs, we as individual men and women are the stewards of the life-begetting potential. No given number of offspring is mandated by God to any of us. God never indicates a requirement as to quantity but only that there be a will to say yes—that we *will* have children, in obedience to His command "Be fruitful . . . multiply."[5]

Contrary to the thinking of some sincere people, the Bible does *not* say birth control is wrong. God has given each of us—mankind—the responsibility of governing the *multiplication* of life. While He *has* commanded us to *beget* children, He has *not* mandated an interminable abandonment to chance *or* required a given number of offspring or assigned us to *in*numerable ones!

What the Bible *does* say, however, is that children are a blessing and should be *sought:*

> Behold, children are a heritage from the LORD, the fruit of the womb is His reward. [6]

The Word of God employs the loveliest terminology in describing the joy of childbirth, the meaningfulness of parenthood and the desirability of a family. But the Bible further implies that since life begins at conception, the willful extinguishing of that life is *not* an acceptable method of birth control. According to God's Word, the frequency of conception *can* be controlled, but life once conceived cannot be taken at human will. In short, (1) man is not to avoid begetting children; (2) man is not to abort those who have been conceived.

So we see from the very establishing of the creative order:

1. God has placed life immediately within man's capacity to reproduce;
2. He has called him to exercise that life-begetting capacity;
3. He clearly expects that once life is conceived, its preciousness will be honored.

We do not need to go to the laboratory to see if life begins at conception, nor are we at the mercy of volatile emotions on the subject. Rather, the cool, crisp words of God's timeless truth show us created man, who from his beginning has possessed the God-given ability to beget another being created like himself. This kind of life is in the loins of *both* the man and the woman since each contributes his or her share toward the multiplication process. In the instant those cells conjoin, another life begins.

Notes
1. See Hebrews 9:27.
2. John 3:7.
3. See John 3:1-12.
4. Genesis 2:7.
5. Genesis 1:28.
6. Psalm 127:3.

CHAPTER 2

WHEN DOES SIGNIFICANCE BEGIN?

God obviously anticipated our inquiry
centuries ahead of time.

Not only does the Bible establish the fact of the prenatal existence of your child as a human being, it further teaches the worth, importance and spiritual viability of every preborn life. David declares this when praising God for how He creates and protects the fetus:

> For You [Lord] formed my inward parts;
> You covered me in my mother's womb. [1]

This text makes direct reference to the deepest part of our being—the "inward parts." The Hebrew term *kilyaw* is the figurative expression used to represent the "foundation of being." Just as we refer to the heart as the seat of our being, or inner person, the Hebrew tongue referred to the kidneys (kilyaw). The use in the Scriptures of this expression, referring to a child in the womb, unquestionably establishes biblical support for the idea that a *spiritual* being, not only a physical one, *does* exist in the womb.

And notice how God's personal attentiveness toward each fetus is so beautifully declared: "You covered me," David announces; that is, "You came to my help." A close scrutiny of the verb chosen by Jewish translators of this passage reveals that the literal statement of the text is that God is *beside* the child—to *help* it and to *keep* it from its earliest beginning.[2]

One can't help but wonder to what David might have been referring. As a child, had his mother told him stories of her being especially protected—sustained by God's intervening grace—during her pregnancy? Might David be saying that he was spared by some providence, or is he simply making a general statement about God's care for the child in the womb? In any case, the inescapable truth is that His personal attention is declared; Jesus strongly affirmed God's personal concern for each individual, noting His very real Creator-care for a mere sparrow and then saying God's care was multiplied for each child, each person, each human being.[3] Psalm 139 gives us mighty insights: (1) God views life in the womb as real and eternal; and (2) God shows us life in the womb is desirable and worth protecting.

WHEN IN THE WOMB DOES LIFE BEGIN?

This question has captured the interest of philosophers and scientists over the centuries, as man has sought to define exactly when life actually begins. More recently, debate has centered on the question as to which trimester—that is, which three-month segment of the nine months of pregnancy—life may in fact become "human."

It seems that God anticipated this specific question ages ago, for in the Bible we have a case in which the most precise evidence is given, showing us that *viable, significant* life in the womb specifically exists during *all* of the first three months; that is, *from conception, fully meaningful life* is present.

Of course, the biologist has shown the poignant physiological evidence of life in the first three months. In the third week, the lobes of the brain are distinguishable; in the fourth week, the head and face are recognizable and the heart starts to beat; during weeks five and six, the eyes are identifiable, and legs are putting on flesh and muscle; in the eighth week, the embryo moves to the fetal stage, and during the following weeks, sex can be identified and the baby can begin to turn its head, squint, frown, make a fist and even get the hiccups: all of this is *before* the end of the first three months in the womb.[4]

As touching as these biological signs of humanity are in the *physical* formation of the child, look with me at the pointed evidence the Bible gives of the *personal, spiritual* viability of that child. An unmistakable statement is present here, as God has placed at the heart of His Word a story which reveals the fact of a baby's real, personal meaning-filled existence during the first three months following conception. It's the story that is among the best known in the world. Although given to tell us of the gift of our Redeemer, hidden within this story is a precious fact concerning the Creator's basic gift of life itself.

Mary, the young woman of Nazareth, has received an angelic visitation announcing her role as the mother of the Messiah. We pick up the story in Luke, chapter 1:

Now Mary arose in those days and went into the hill country with haste, to a city of Judah, and entered the house of Zacharias and greeted Elizabeth. And it happened, when Elizabeth heard the greeting of Mary, that the babe leaped in her womb; and Elizabeth was filled with the Holy Spirit. Then she spoke out with a loud voice and said, "Blessed are you among women, and blessed is the fruit of your womb! But why is this granted to me, that the mother of my Lord should come to me?" [5]

The words of Mary's cousin Elizabeth are astonishingly relevant to the philosophical inquiry of this twentieth century. The precision of the text seems crafted by the Holy Spirit twenty centuries in advance. Within the span of 20 verses in Luke's Gospel (1:26-56), we are explicitly told that

- a child has been conceived in Mary's womb;
- the child is present, alive, and "the Lord" at the moment—no less a person for being a fetus; and
- the exact chronology of the events.

In verse 36, the angel told Mary at the same time as *her* conception, that Elizabeth was in her sixth month of pregnancy. In verse 56, we are told Mary stayed with her until the birth of Elizabeth's baby: "And Mary remained with her about three months." In other words, when Elizabeth was filled with the Holy Spirit and prophesied upon Mary's arrival—the child in your womb is the

Lord—Mary was only a matter of a few days into *her* pregnancy.

It's astounding.

It's a prophetic statement cut from the cloth of human experience two millennia ago and unrolled before mankind today. Does the Bible say that life in its truest essence exists from conception?

Absolutely!

Does it specifically answer questions about the first trimester of pregnancy?

Absolutely!

And the most profound revelation to the thoughtful reader and inquirer should be *not* in the fact the question is answered but in the manifest fact that God obviously anticipated our

> *A* human—
> *a lasting, eternal soul—*
> *is present*
> *from conception.*

inquiry centuries ahead of time. The meticulous detail, written without strain to the natural flow of the story, silences the doubts of any who accept the authority of God's Holy Word: Life—personal life, meaningful life, *human* life in its deepest, lasting sense—exists in the womb from conception. We are not only shown the evidence of a real body in the formation during the first trimester, but we are also given a conclusive statement concerning a real *being* at the same time: a *human*—a lasting, eternal soul—is present from conception.

THE POINT IS PERMANENCE

And what is the point of this exercise in Bible exegesis? Simply this: to establish a foundation for the *permanent* existence of the child you lost through stillbirth, miscarriage, abortion or infant death.

Your child *still* exists! Your child not only *was* a real, valid, meaningful person from the moment of his or her conception, but he or she has *continued* to be a real, lasting eternal being since the moment of his or her death.

- A miscarried child does not disappear as a being simply because a clump of tissue slipped from its grip in the womb.

- An aborted baby does not cease his or her larger existence simply because a surgical instrument or vacuum scraped or sucked the baby's physical existence into oblivion.
- And to the parent of the stillborn or to those who have held a dead baby in their arms—one who died so shortly after birth, seeming to have flown before it was truly known, caught away by an early flight—I tell you, that child's soul (and the same with the miscarried and aborted) is no less caught up to God's presence as an eternal being than the soul of a ninety-year-old man or woman, who dies and goes to their Maker.

The Word of God, the Creator's handbook for humanity, gives us understanding at this initial point of inquiry: What about the reality of life of the blastula, the embryo, the fetus, the stillborn? His answer: *It's real.* And therein a biblical point of hope is present, for this means that your lost child is in God's presence, and you will someday meet him or her.

For Some, a Dilemma

But I can almost hear someone asking, "What if the child I will someday meet in heaven is one that I made a choice to abort? Will he or she accuse me of disallowing him or her life as I have been allowed it?"

What a poignant question.

What a potentially haunting specter: to arrive in the afterworld, to stand in the presence of God and to be indicted *not* only by the Almighty Himself, but by a being never really known yet, in that moment, completely recognized. How unimaginable, to have that person rise, point to you and say, "That is the one who bore me—and the one who denied me life on Earth." What a stark, raw, emotion-shattering scene! Could such a moment be?

On the ground of God's Word, the answer is *never*!

NEVER!

Any judgment before God's throne will be declared by Him alone. He will not marshal witnesses against us, for it is solely with Him we have to deal when we give our accounting, and He is the faithful witness of all our lives. [6]

Furthermore, the fear of recrimination for *any* sin or failure *never* needs to cloud your soul, because the greatest fact in the universe is God's provision for *all* of our forgiveness:

> For God so loved the world that He gave His only begotten Son, that whoever believes in Him should not perish but have everlasting life.[7]

And your or my relative undeservedness of such merciful love and great forgiveness is not an obstacle:

> But God demonstrates His own love toward us, in that while we were still sinners, Christ died for us.[8]

The happy and holy consequence of Christ's death for our sins is that complete payment has been made and complete forgiveness is fully available to you and me today.

I run a very real risk by examining, in this manner, the heartache of abortion and the path to healing. It is entirely possible that someone may misjudge my desire to comfort, concluding that correction is needed instead. But my effort is not prompted by a casual attitude toward the fact that fetuses are being killed. Instead, I am driven by the realization that most mothers who choose abortion are not indifferent to the child within. If an abortion lurks in your past, your choice was promoted and encouraged by a society temporarily numbed to the truest values of human life. While this societal influence does not lessen the magnitude of your personal choice, let me ask you this: Which one of us is free from the ramifications and pain inflicted by our sinful choices? The glimmering hope of one and all is that Jesus Himself reaches in tenderness to each of us in the aftermath of our own hurtful decisions and brings good news to broken people.

Let me ask you something—and it's not merely if you've felt shame, guilt or stain because of your part in an abortion. Indeed, even if abortion is not one of the failures in your past, every one of us has sinned. Total honesty before God brings with it a sense of condemnation for choices in our past, as well as factors still very much a part of the present. Is this how you feel? Is there something in your past or in your present that cries out to be admitted and abandoned, confessed, cleansed and forgiven?

Listen. There's good news today.

God's provisions for our past are not only sufficient, but His promise for our future is also incredibly bright! A brilliant light shines from

> *A brilliant light shines from the face of Jesus, burning away the darkness of sinshadows which seek to engulf each soul.*

the face of Jesus, not only burning away the darkness of sinshadows which seek to engulf the soul, but also radiating a beam of brightness into the future.

Open your heart to Him—to His love, hope and comfort: "But as many as received Him, to them He gave the right to become children of God."[9] If you've never asked forgiveness for past sin, *of any* or *every* kind; or if you've never invited our Savior Jesus Christ to enter your life in healing love and saving power, do it now.

Prayerfully bow and speak your heart cry to Him.

After doing so, in the spirit of peace which His healing truth and love can bring, questions about those little ones who have taken the early flight will be answered by a new level of hope, elevated by the fact that your soul has had its greatest need supplied: a Savior.

If you have never personally welcomed the Lord Jesus into your heart, to be *your* Savior and to lead you in the matters of *your* life, I would like to encourage and help you to do that.

There is no need to delay, for an honest heart can approach the loving Father God at any time. So I'd like to invite you to come with me and let's pray to Him right now.

If it's possible, where you are, bow your head—or even kneel. In either case, read my simple prayer first, and then pray using the words below the subhead "Your Prayer."

MY PRAYER

Father God, I have the privilege of joining with this child of Yours who is reading this book right now.

I want to thank You for the openness of heart being shown toward You and I want to praise You for Your promise: when we call to You, You will answer.

I know that genuine sincerity is present in this heart, which is ready to speak this prayer, so we come to You in the name and through the Cross of Your Son, the Lord Jesus. Thank You for hearing.

YOUR PRAYER

Dear God, I am doing this because I believe in Your love for me, and I want to ask You to come to me as I come to You. Please help me now.

First, I thank You for sending Your Son, Jesus, to Earth to live and to die for me on the cross. I thank You for the gift of forgiveness of sin that You offer me now, and I pray for that forgiveness.

Forgive me and cleanse my life in Your sight, through the blood of Jesus Christ. I am sorry for anything and everything I have ever done that is unworthy in Your sight. Please take away all guilt and shame, as I accept the fact that Jesus died to pay for all my sins and through Him, I am now given forgiveness on this earth and eternal life in heaven.

I ask You, Lord Jesus, please come into my life now. Because You rose from the dead, I know You're

alive and I want You to live with me—now and forever.
I am turning my life over to You and from my
way to Yours. I invite Your Holy Spirit to fill me and
lead me forward in a life that will please
the heavenly Father.
Thank You for hearing me. From this day forward,
I commit myself to Jesus Christ, the Son of God.
In His name, amen.[10]

Notes

1. Psalm 139:13.
2. Septuagint: *antilambano.*
3. See Matthew 10:31.
4. *LIFE* magazine reprint, copyright 1965, 1979.
5. Luke 1:39-43.
6. See 2 Corinthians 5:10 and Hebrews 4:13.
7. John 3:16.
8. Romans 5:8.
9. John 1:12.
10. If you have received Jesus Christ as your Savior, it would be my pleasure to send you a gift copy of my book, concerning how a newborn believer in Christ can grow. Please remove the page at the end of the book, fill in the address information, and mail to me. Your decision will be held in confidence, we will pray for you, and you will be sent a copy of *NEWBORN: Your New Life with Christ* (Tyndale House Publishers, 1987).

CHAPTER 3

LIFE TO WHAT DEGREE?

Our investigation of such questions must be more than merely theoretical or theological; and in making the Creator's Handbook our textbook, we have substance, not theory.

In the light of God's eternal Word, we have established that life does indeed begin at conception—that even before birth, a fully significant being has begun its realization of the Creator's purpose for its own self.

In discussing the aborted, miscarried and stillborn, another question rises:

> Since the body never reaches completion
>   (as with the miscarried or aborted);
> since it never grows beyond birth (as with
>   the stillborn);
> since those lips never cried, much less spoke
>   intelligibly;
> since that tininess hardly thought reflec-
>   tively or made a self-conscious assessment
>   of its own being; then,
> what is the exact nature of that undevel-
>   oped eternal being?

The popular consensus would be that your child never was, or if he or she *was* somehow, no longer *is*. The natural deduction of the mind unenlightened by divine revelation is that the infant life so sadly wasted, either by physical malfunction or decisive human intervention, could never realize a destiny—indeed, probably never had one. But just as ignorance forfeits hope, insight can regain it.

We have already found that each child has, before birth, a divinely ordained endlessness to his or her being: Humankind once conceived become eternal souls, since life does not begin with the first breath or the first heartbeat. It begins with the initial uniting of the cells contributed by the mother and the father. From that moment, according to the Bible, a viable being exists—a being that transcends its relative physical durability, whether that is eight hours within the womb or eighty years beyond it.

This being God's conclusive word on the subject, we may logically ask: What is the eternal destiny of the unborn, stillborn or early-death child? If the child never knew a life on Earth, what becomes of him or her? What purpose? What intelligence has the child? Indeed, the child may be eternal but an eternal "what"? To what degree does this life exist?

GROUNDS FOR UNDERSTANDING

Our investigation of such questions must be more than merely theoretical or theological; and in making the Creator's Handbook our textbook, we have substance, not theory. We are not guessing, for God's Word of truth eliminates guesswork. Neither are we theologizing for the sake of academic argument. God didn't give His Word as a text for forming ritual creeds but as a source for answering human need.

God has given us insights in His Word that can conquer our fears.

Our foremost need is to know God's love and forgiveness, but with this we also need the hope He extends. Only His Word offers the pathway to discovery of His purpose—a functional purpose that brings both meaning to our lives and strength to rise above our weaknesses. God has given insights in His Word that can conquer our fears, bringing lasting hope that our failures or disappointments need not preempt our possibilities.

This is what God's program of redemption is about: the restoration of life *and hope*.

Redemption has a triple focus: (1) God redeems our past; (2) God provides hope and power for our present experiences, offering a beautiful and fulfilling life *now*; (3) God promises us eternal joy in heaven. The second point is too often misunderstood. He forgives us to give us a future, and He redeems us to begin a program of restoring all that we have lost, whether through our helplessness, ignorance, neglect, failure or sin.

Thus, with direct reference to the subject of the destiny of those little ones who have taken early flight from this world, we have reason for great expectation. Examination of the solid ground of the Scriptures gives footing for faith in a future beyond our heartaches. To determine exactly what your early flight child may be or become beyond the womb, we must answer the following questions:

- Is that being—your child—sensitive and responsive as a spiritual entity? Is there evidence that he or she possesses insight or intellect in the most spiritual sense of the word?
- If so, is there a positive eternal destiny ensured for these children we never knew? What of heaven? Where in heaven? Or, heaven at all?

The Bible is anything but silent about the spiritual nature of these little ones and yet I have never heard any teaching concerning these questions. I confess, I would never have begun this quest to probe these passages were it not for two factors.

First, as a pastor of a large, growing urban congregation, I was repeatedly encountering believers, newly born again to faith in Jesus Christ, whose memories contained the pain of their past related to abortion. They wondered about the life of the one they had extinguished from this planet.

Second, an unusual and very interesting conversation took place. Let me tell you the story.

One day my wife, Anna, and I were talking with an older lady, a dear saint who had been part of our congregation for many years. Over the years we had come to know her as both a sensitive and sensible person. Except for the fact that she was such a balanced, spiritually minded, scripturally ordered person, we probably would not have been ready to put much stock in the episode she related. In a nonmystical, very natural and unaffected way, she recounted the following:

> Shortly after my husband and I had our first child, I became pregnant again.

Because we were so young, because it was during the Depression and because neither of us knew Christ nor God's Word of promise, we sought and I experienced an abortion. Some years later, after our other children were fully grown, I was at prayer one day—not even thinking of this long-past fact of our lives—when the Holy Spirit said: "You have never presented that child to the Father." I was quite taken aback, not because I felt shamed or condemned, but because I hadn't even been thinking about that abortion experience. Second, it would *never* have occurred to me to *ever* make an actual dedication of an aborted child to God.

Still, the experience being so clear, I spoke with my husband about it, and after prayer and studying the Word of God, we did exactly that—we dedicated our child together. We knew we had long since been forgiven for the sin we shared at that time, in our ignorance of God's better way. But now we simply prayed: "Lord, You are the Father of all spirits. Your Word says so, and we believe You not only gave us an eternal soul whose body we mistreated in our ignorance but whose being still exists within Your great domain. Knowing nothing more, we humbly come to present this child You gave us—to present it to You. And we do this in Jesus' name, amen."

Now, that couple did *not* feel that prayer was accomplishing some "salvation by proxy" or any such foolish notion. Nor were they presenting a new doctrine or some pattern of behavior they felt should be observed by everyone who shared their particular failure. To the contrary, they simply were responding to something they felt within their own hearts. That act of dedication was not so much for the baby's benefit as for their own, for the experience helped them to a genuine realization that their baby still exists—something they had not considered as deeply before.

As for me, hearing that episode prodded me into a diligent study of the Scriptures. As a result, I was not only moved, edified and enlightened by the Word as I pursued this theme for teaching the congregation; but since then, I have shared these truths with countless numbers via the media.

A Glimpse from Jeremiah

Now we come to the question of the *spiritual* capacity of the unborn child. Begin with me at the words of the prophet Jeremiah.

> Before I formed you in the womb I knew you; before you were born I sanctified you.[1]

Although it is clear in the text that Jeremiah is specifically speaking about God's Word to him personally, the Bible is equally clear that God is no respecter of persons. He is as committed to *each* of us as He is to *any* of us, and it is with that understanding that our glimpse from Jeremiah becomes a look at God's view of each of us—while we were yet unborn.

The prophet pointedly attests to God's revelation that man's prenatal existence is linked to a postnatal one; in other words, the life of our soul is an eternal, spiritual continuum that begins at conception and continues through and beyond birth. Just as our body experiences a *temporal* physical continuum that begins in the womb and continues to grow and function beyond it for our *earthly* lifetime, so our spirit—the essence of our life—exists from conception and beyond for our *eternal* lifetime.

While notably underscoring the ongoing spiritual viability of the child who never experiences life outside the womb, this verse yields two facts about *every* human: (1) divine intent, or purpose; and (2) divine input, or provision.

Intent and Purpose

The words "Before I formed you in the womb I knew you" do not suggest the preexistence of the personality, but they do teach God's preawareness of intent for the child. He is saying for each of us to understand, "None of you is an accident. I have foreknown your conception. I have preplanned and provided purpose for your life." To personally apply the essence of this concept can be mightily transforming for any one of us.

In private counsel I have met so many people whose sense of personal worth was repeatedly demeaned during their childhood by such remarks as "We never planned on you" or "If we had known what we were doing, we would have had fewer children." Such depersonalizing feelings are often accentuated when people discover they are illegitimate offspring or the product of an extramarital affair. Individuals question their worth, despair over their destiny and often succumb to feelings of pointlessness—especially in a society that argues for *chance* as the explanation of man's creation rather than God's *purpose*.

But to all human fear, blindness and misgiving, God speaks from His Word. He was not caught by surprise where *any* of us were concerned! "Before you were formed in the womb I knew you." Let that deep statement of His primary intent and purpose for every human being seep into *your* soul, and let it be a hallmark of our awareness about each child in the womb. Whatever the frustration, inconvenience, pain or displeasure, there is no being without purpose in the larger providences of God. His purposes may not always harmonize with ours, but in the eternal symphony, we will come to recognize better the part played by each creature—even when the note played by circumstances seems dissonant.

Input and Provision

Jeremiah 1:5 illustrates that God's purpose for people is already in force—in His mind and intent—while they are in the womb. "I ordained you a prophet to the nations," God said of Jeremiah; and in respect to a planned purpose, he is not an exception; he is an example of God's intent. He is proof that no unborn child is without distinct spiritual significance in God's design.

But there is a second feature in this text, for in saying to Jeremiah "I ordained you a prophet," God is not merely making an assignment, He is ensuring a sufficiency. He assigns duty, but He also gives the ability to accomplish it.

The implied message is that inherent in every child is not only the *promise* of God's purpose but the *provision* of God's power to accomplish that purpose. I feel particularly moved to point that out because I have known of people tempted to abort a child through their unawareness of the dual truth this verse reveals. They not only haven't realized that God already has a *purpose* for the child, but they also don't know God's *promise* of provision. Without hope or faith that He will provide for and help them see that child's purpose realized, fear and unbelief take over. I have even known of abortions performed simply because of fears of economic failure in the practical task of parenthood.

But God has a promise for such a person: If you'll let His purpose be realized in the child you may fear having, He'll help you at every point.

Ask Him for wisdom and claim His promises to provide an adequate supply for material or monetary need. Ask and you will receive—and your joy in your children shall be full!

SPIRITUALLY SENSITIVE?

Is the unborn child a viable, real spiritual entity—a creature with God's purpose and power in beginning measure, a being with a sensitivity to the Almighty and His designs?

A classic case in evidence takes us back again to the Gospel of Luke, but this time we consider another baby, John the Baptist, who was in his mother Elizabeth's womb. The same passage we read earlier amplifies our understanding on yet another point.[2]

With the arrival of Mary, within whom the Messiah, Jesus, had already been conceived, the child within Elizabeth is prompted to *leap*—literally jump in response to the present reality that was in the person of the yet unborn Christ. This is incredibly significant since an angel had prophesied of John the Baptist to his father Zacharias, "He [John the Baptist] will also go before Him in the spirit and power of Elijah [that is, before the

Messiah to announce His presence]."[3] Amazingly, in fact it's almost humorous, the baby seems to be doing precisely that! What John would be doing with intelligent speech and by reason of spiritual cognizance 30 years later beside the Jordan River, he first does as an unborn child!

The small human mass within the womb is already tuned to the Spirit of his or her maker.

This is more than an interesting coincidence: The baby wasn't just happy to jump. Rather, Elizabeth's own testimony attributes her certainty of God's witness to the occasion as being directly related to the baby's leaping within her. Man may call it superstition and we might be tempted to call it coincidental, but the Bible says it was the Holy Spirit at work.

Let no one say the unborn are without spiritual sensitivity or purpose. Intelligence may not have flowered yet nor speech have been acquired, but a purpose has already been plotted by the

Creator. The small human mass within the womb is already tuned to the Spirit of his or her maker.

In Dr. Thomas Verney's book *The Secret Life of the Unborn Child*, he notes the difference in the fetus's response, even as early as four and a half months, if either iodine or sugar is injected into the amniotic fluid of the womb. The child reacts disagreeably to the taste of iodine but drinks at twice the normal rate of consumption if sugar is present. Verney goes on to say that unborn children react to the emotional charges they receive from the mother, noting that if the mother is really looking forward to the pregnancy, "it has an incredible, positive effect" on the baby.[4]

We are unhesitant to acknowledge that the evidence is in, as far as the natural realm is concerned. Let us be neither surprised to discover nor hesitant to acknowledge that the Bible tells us an unborn child is at least equally responsive and sensitive to the spiritual realm as well.

Notes
1. Jeremiah 1:5.
2. See Luke 1:39-43.
3. Luke 1:17.
4. Thomas Verney, *The Secret Life of the Unborn Child* (London: Time Warner Books, UK, 1988), n.p.

CHAPTER 4

DESTINY IN THE AFTERWORLD

*Man without a Savior is an eternally
perishable being.*

We've established that the prenatal child is an eternal being capable of spiritual response. Now we ask, If a child dies before or shortly after birth, what is his or her destiny in the afterworld?

At once, we open the question of options in the hereafter. Human philosophy suggests numerous possibilities, but God advises there are only two. Man's reasonings offer everything from oblivion to euphoria, from nothingness to anythingness, from extinction like a worm dried on the pavement to an indeterminate number of incarnations as a being moves from one life to another. But God says that once concluded on Earth, human life proceeds to either heaven or hell.

No limbo.

No nirvana.

No purgatory.

No reincarnation.

No oblivion.

God's Word describes either (1) a destiny *within* His will and desire or (2) a destiny resulting from *opposing* His will and desire. That these are the only options—eternal gain or eternal loss—is the only fact that gives credence to the extreme measure God's love required to ensure the possibility that each person can receive the promise of heaven.

God so loved the world that He gave His
only begotten Son, that whoever believes
in Him should not perish but have ever-
lasting life.[1]

Man without a Savior is an eternally perishable
being. That "perish" is *not* nothingness but the endless suffering of a created soul separated from its
Creator by its own choice and sin.

The apostle Paul elaborates the depth of this
fact, accentuating again how the passion of Jesus
Christ, who admittedly came and died essentially
to rescue a truly lost humanity, verifies the reality and awfulness of the lostness of mankind.

For the love of Christ constrains us,
because we judge thus: that if One died
for all, then all died; and He died for all,
that those who live should live no longer
for themselves, but for Him who died for
them and rose again.[2]

The entire motive in Jesus Christ's coming was
the love of our Creator who refuses to allow any of
us—His own creation—to perish without the availability of a way back from sin's self-initiated exile.

God's goal is to bring us back *into* the present fulfillment He offers and unto the eternal joy He created us to know.

With the fact of limited options in the after-world established in God's Word, what does He reveal concerning the disposition of the unborn and stillborn at their death?

TO HEAVEN OR . . . ?

Our hearts dictate "Heaven, of course!" And as true as that may well be, our answer must derive from greater authority than convictions based solely on our emotions. Doubtless we would all argue for their being instantly ushered into the Creator's heaven-home forever. And that answer *is* right, but we need grounds superior to our own human sense of justice. We need an authoritative statement from the judge of the universe. What will He say?

With regard to these little ones, as with every human being coming before His presence at his or her passing, we can rest assured: *God is just.* He does not need any prompting from our emotional or rational proposals. Our insistence that surely or of course those unborn are saved is unnecessary here. God knows the spirit of the rebellious, and that cosmic cul-de-sac called Hell

> *Their early departure*
> *from life here takes them*
> *immediately into*
> *His presence.*

is only a self-imposed place of endless abandonment for people who reject Him. Thus, unsurprisingly, His Word *is* clear concerning these sinless little ones: Their early departure from life here takes them immediately into His presence. And our hope can rest in that knowledge on the rock of His Word, not merely on our feelings.

GOD'S WORDS ON DEAD INFANTS

Jesus' Words

It is with great tenderness that Jesus speaks of the innocence of little children: "Their angels always see the face of My Father."[3] His meaning is clearly that—notwithstanding every child's inherent potential for sinning—small children, still in their innocence, enjoy an uninterrupted discourse with the heart of God. At what age this is broken cannot be measured, for it would vary with each person. Still, one thing is clear: An unborn or stillborn child hasn't transgressed that union.

David's Song

In the Old Testament, David spoke of his departed son, who died but days after birth: "I shall go to him"[4] This statement is broadened in its significance when we note that it was spoken by the same lips which sang, "And I will dwell in the house of the LORD forever."[5] The place of eternal dwelling for the child now gone was known to be the same place anticipated by the believer who has received God's promise and redemption.

Abraham's Cry

When God told Abraham He was going to destroy Sodom and Gomorrah, Abraham asked, "Would You also destroy the righteous with the wicked?"[6] He seems to be appealing to God in the interest of the innocent. Then, he apparently remembers that He doesn't need to goad God to do good, and he answers his own question, "Far be it from You to do such a thing as this, to slay the righteous

with the wicked, so that the righteous should be as the wicked; far be it from You! Shall not the Judge of all the earth do right?"[7]

Yes! A thousand times, yes! The judge of the earth *can* be counted on *always*. He will do justice. He will do right. Always!

As with Abraham and with us and our children, God is fair on *heaven's* terms, not merely Earth's. And in those eternal, abiding policies, the message of the Word teaches that the stillborn, the newly born who die, the miscarried and the aborted do indeed pass into the presence of God.

What About the Unsaved?

But what if the parents are not believers? Doesn't the Bible say something about the child then being outside God's grace as I have described?

This question is probably raised on the basis of a misunderstanding of 1 Corinthians 7:14: "For the unbelieving husband is sanctified by the wife, and the unbelieving wife is sanctified by the husband; otherwise your children would be unclean, but now they are holy."

But this passage has nothing to do with the spiritual viability of the offspring of a spiritually mixed couple or of an unsaved couple.

In this text, the apostle Paul is addressing a moral question. The Corinthians were wondering about the legitimacy of children born to a couple where only one person confessed Christ as Savior. Was the couple's relationship impure, unholy—and thereby their children illegal or unsanctified—in God's eyes? Paul's answer is swift and direct: "No, the children are in no way reduced in God's eyes"; they are declared socially and legally acceptable in God's sight. But in saying this, the Bible neither declares nor implies that parents determine the eternal destiny of their children. Believing couples do not automatically produce believing children, and conversely, the nonbelief of unbelieving parents does not automatically doom their children to eternal loss.

Salvation is always an individual choice. Parental influence during the child's lifetime does contribute positively or negatively, but it cannot control it. As to the destiny of the unborn, since the children have made no moral choices, they have remained innocent. Thereby God's perfect justice receives them into His presence, irrespective of the spiritual condition of the parents—and without consideration of what the circumstance of the child's conception may have been.

After reading all of this, the following questions may arise:

- Why does so much confusion, misunderstanding and condemnation surround us?
- Why do so many people wonder about purpose in their lives?
- Why does fear win over faith, and why are babies snuffed out in the womb like candles in the wind?
- Why does guilt successfully maintain its grip over so many in spite of the fact that God's forgiveness is so freely offered?
- Why does smallness of spirit compel believers to sit in judgment of human failure rather than to minister comfort and hope?

The answers to these questions are summarily handled and answered in one direct statement from Jesus:

The thief does not come except to steal, and to kill, and to destroy.[8]

According to Christ, precisely what we are addressing is the work of the devil—a satanic *theft* of joy, a demonic *killing* of hope and a hellish *destruction* of lives. But the solution to mastery over our archopponent's workings is in Jesus' ensuing words:

> I have come that they may have life, and that they may have it more abundantly.[9]

Here is truth: The child of early flight—the still-born, the newborn who dies, the miscarried, the aborted—is not a "nothing" that has gone nowhere.

- He or she was not just a small wad of cells washed down a drain. He or she was not just a mass of bones and tissue thrown into a plastic bag.
- He or she is not a stiffened corpse laid in a small coffin.

Rather, each of those little ones are present with the Father. They have identity and individuality, and they deserve to be known for what they are—eternal beings. They still have a divine purpose which, though it may transcend our understanding for the moment, we shall perceive clearly when the day dawns that we no longer see as through a glass, darkly but then face-to-face.[10]

If comfort is what you need, I want to touch your hand. I want to pour the oil of hope into your heart if the flame has flickered and needs fuel to brighten tomorrow.

My friend, the truth can set you free—and the truth with which we deal is the Holy Spirit's key to your release. Whatever your heart calls for, whether remote to the immediate subject or directly in the center of it, let's call to Jesus Himself. He is the Truth incarnate and readily present. Invite His working into every facet of your present moment with your heartfelt prayer: *Come, Lord Jesus.*

Notes
1. John 3:16.
2. 2 Corinthians 5:14-15.
3. Matthew 18:10.
4. 2 Samuel 12:23.
5. Psalm 23:6.
6. Genesis 18:23.
7. Genesis 18:25.
8. John 10:10.
9. John 10:10.
10. See 1 Corinthians 13:12.

CHAPTER 5

IN HEAVEN AS
A PERSON

*Now there are heavenly bodies and there are earthly bodies
and the glory of each is different from the other.*

(SEE 1 CORINTHIANS 15:40.)

To summarize, we have examined these truths from the Bible as they relate to your son or daughter lost through death:

- From conception, life not only is truly human but also is thereby truly an endless being. An eternal soul exists.
- Each unborn being has viable spiritual sensitivity. Although intellect and speech as we know it may not have begun, sensitivity, spiritual potential and distinctly human capacities are present.
- God places inestimable value on and has planned purpose for every human life, so much so that He gave His Son to recover from eternal loss all who will receive His redemption.
- The unborn, stillborn or infant at death does immediately pass into the presence of God; i.e., the child goes to heaven.

The sum of these statements is that the aborted, miscarried, stillborn or early-death child *exists*; he or she is with God as an eternal soul and is capable of spiritual, sensitive communication. But still another question reasonably comes to mind.

If the unborn child having died does actually go to heaven, in what form does he or she appear there? Since the child never developed beyond an embryo or fetus, how would the child appear in heaven? And even a stillborn child, though usually physically complete, generally has little distinct physical identification. How does the child look in eternity?

Are such questions important?

I think so, because we are *all* creatures destined for eternity. Incorporated in God's presence in that eternal city will be all those beings who left before birth, as well as all of us who survived for a life span beyond it. We will meet one another there, and we will meet those infants. Once the horizons of that perspective open up, they may garner for each of us a host of biblically based values.

Here God's Word shines again as it so often does in the dark night of human pain. Consider what it says about a possible *meeting* with the child that left you before or shortly after birth.

A Meeting Someday

In the Old Testament, a marvelously tender story appears—a factual piece of history that climaxes a case of failure with a hope-filled promise. You've heard the story.[1]

> From the balcony of his home, David sees his neighbor Uriah's wife bathing. Filled with lust, he orders Bathsheba to his room and makes love to her, while her warrior husband is away at battle, serving the very man who is taking his wife. The sordid details of the story result in Bathsheba's pregnancy, Uriah's murder and David's indictment by Nathan the prophet. "The child shall not live," Nathan declares.
>
> Shortly after birth, the baby begins to decline—death seems imminent. David seeks God's mercy with repentance, fasting and prayer, refusing food in order to intercede before God in behalf of the child.
>
> When the child dies, David is not embittered, resentful or mournful. His servants are bewildered as he rises from prayer and ceases his mourning. And there, against that ancient backdrop of human ignorance about God's higher

purposes for children who have died, David speaks the word of revelation—the word of God's truth: "I shall go to him, but he shall not return to me."[2]

Take special note of these words.

They are spoken by a man who sinned. Let us especially see how God-given hope springs in the breast of the very person who is in fact charged with being the *reason* the child didn't survive! But he is also a person who both lamented his failure and repented of it. And now he's speaking with hope: "I shall go to him."

You are specifically freed to expect to meet your child in heaven.

David lived a long life following this episode, but here he is saying: "The day will come when I will meet that child, will greet that child and will some day forever be with that child."

That's in the Bible, friend. This isn't myth, fable, legend or a selection of poetic thoughts for the sorrowful. This is truth to set us free. Here you are specifically freed to expect to meet your child in heaven, to recognize him or her and to be with your child.

HOW SHALL THEY APPEAR?

"But, Jack," I can almost hear somebody say, "what about the miscarried and aborted babies? How do they appear? How could I know or recognize them? In what form are they?"

Thankfully, the Word of God provides us with enough information that those are answerable questions, too. Although David was referring to a baby who died a few days after it was born, we can authoritatively answer concerning even a miscarried embryo, which may have been only weeks along the way toward birth.

From 1 Corinthians 15 we gain our first footing:

> Now there are heavenly bodies and there are earthly bodies, and the glory of each is different from the other (see v. 40).

The Bible makes it clear: people who have departed Earth are not wispy spooks, blowing in the wind. Satanic deceptions employ such ghost-ly projections and are practiced by occultists who conjure up horrifying demonic presences that delude, blind and purvey fear. But the few times we see people in the Bible who, to use the scrip-tural term, are in their "heavenly bodies," they are identifiable.

When the disciples on the Mount of Trans-figuration saw Jesus talking with Moses and Elijah, they recognized them as human beings and intu-itively knew who they were. They didn't witness double exposure-type pictures, nor were they struck dumb or horrified by ectoplasmic mirages. They saw *people* who had died. The Bible in fact dis-tinctly mentions Moses' burial; and Elijah's experi-ence, though unusual, did not preempt actual physical death. Of course, the disciples had never before seen Elijah and Moses, yet they knew imme-diately who they were.

But how will I recognize someone who never had a body?

This is not only a reasonable question, but it also is a difficult one. After all, if the miscarried or aborted child was not even completely formed at the time of his or her passing, what is there to meet or to greet?

GOD'S RECORD OF YOUR APPEARANCE

Psalm 139 is an ode to the wonder of God's genius and love in providing us with the incredibly marvelous equipment we call the human body. In verses 15 and 16, the psalmist writes, "My frame was not hidden from You, when I was made in secret, and skillfully wrought in the lowest parts of the earth. Your eyes saw my substance, being yet unformed. And in Your book they all were written, the days fashioned for me, when as yet there were none of them."

Here, 30 centuries ago, is fantastic advance notice of something we have only begun to understand today. The writer is saying, "Lord, all my members are written in your book, even while I was being formed in the womb, You already have a record of what I shall become physically." *The New English Bible* puts it with this crystal clarity: "Thou didst see my limbs unformed in the womb, and in thy book they are all recorded; day by day they were fashioned, not one of them was late in growing."[3]

To which "book" does the Bible refer? Where is the book that lists the details of each one of our body's personal design and detailed development?

As recently as the 1950s, two biologists won the Nobel Prize for discovering the secret of DNA, the spiraling double helix within the cellular structure of the human body that holds in coded form the details of every aspect of each person's physical potential. What's remarkable is this book, so to speak, is within every *cell*—the *whole* blueprint. This means, essentially, that even in the smallest collection of cells formulating the tissue of a miscarried child, the encoded message of his or her physical development and appearance-to-be is already present. In short, God knows what your unborn baby would have looked like when he or she was 12 or when he or she was 28.

This information isn't intended to answer every question, for there are some we can only speculate on at the present. But what I have said is not speculation. We are dealing in these certainties:

- The child you lost has a human physical form and is not an airy ghost floating somewhere in space.

- You will meet him or her some day and will simply and immediately "know" who they are, for we will be in the era when we will know as we are known.[4]
- The physical form is as unpredictable to you now as it was before birth but is very possibly like the body his or her genetic code would have dictated had the child lived.

God's Word is amazing, isn't it!
Just like His grace.

Notes
1. See 2 Samuel 11—12.
2. 2 Samuel 12:23.
3. Psalm 139:16, *NEB*.
4. See 1 Corinthians 13:9-12.

CHAPTER 6

INSTRUMENTS OF HEALING

All truth is for action, not merely for meditation.

The statements on the previous pages are consistent with biblical revelation.

We aren't guessing.

And in the light of all we have discovered, the question naturally should occur: What should I do about all of this? All truth is for action, not merely for meditation. Because God reveals His will in His Word to direct us, not merely to inform us, His Word is designed to assist us to a response that aligns us with His will. One certainty is that He wants us all to become instruments of love, His life and His healing, and I want to invite you to take some steps along that pathway.

UNDERSTANDING THE TRUTH ABOUT GOD

The truths we've studied have to do with the removal of the confusion surrounding the destiny of the unborn or newly born who are lost through death. The Word shows their significance, purpose and eternal potential, and holds forth the certainty that these children shall have physical forms in the world to come. The Bible offers the prospect of a new world, a new togetherness, a new dimension of relationship.

There is a verse of Scripture that is often quoted, and it's amazing what some have done with it! Some people clip off the beginning and forget the end. We say: "All things work together for good." Some of the time, the verse is quoted with a *que sera sera* attitude, a passive stance that suggests "What will be, will be," as though we are helpless victims of God's sovereign will who, whatever happens, just have to hope for the best.

But that's not what this verse says. There's a certainty in it: "And we know that all things work together for good to those who love God, to those who are the called according to His purpose."[1] What the passage is really saying is that no matter how our soul's enemy attacks or human circumstances impact our lives, God can ultimately take the pain or problem, redeem it and use it for our good. What Satan planned for evil, God can use for good.

It's possible that coping with the loss of your child has led you down a path of bitterness and anger.

But your loss wasn't God's fault. We live in a broken, imperfect world, and we are members of a fallen race. The residual fallout of the Fall continually appears around us in the form of sickness, sin, natural disaster, tragedy and death. If, however, you make God the focus of your frustration, you not only fail to receive the comfort He can give, but you also are wasting emotional energy by aiming your anger at the wrong target.

EMBRACE THE PROCESS OF GRIEF

The attitude of many bystanders toward the loss of a child through miscarriage, abortion, stillbirth or death shortly after birth can sometimes verge on outright insensitivity. You probably know the kind of people I'm talking about. These people may have responded to your child as a nonentity, particularly if the child died in the womb before you had a chance to actually physically hold and touch that new little life. These same people may have downplayed your grief, leading you to feel abnormal for experiencing deep grief and a sense of loss for the baby you never really got to know.

Please be comforted. Just as Scripture has evidenced the reality and significance of the life once nurtured in your womb, your loss is also real and significant. Don't be surprised if you

experience the same general cycle of grief as anyone who has lost a loved one. Indeed, the depth of
feeling may not be as great or the season of grief
as prolonged, because there are few, if any, memories to deal with. But so often there are *dreams*
that became unfulfilled and anticipated *joy* that
was suddenly quenched.

As soon as you found out about your pregnancy, did your heart begin to love and encom-
pass that new little life? Though you didn't know
your child, did his or her early flight leave a vacuum in your heart? Let none of us ever be surprised or embarrassed by such deep emotions
over the passing of an unborn child. The loss is a
real one. And when grief is present, it needs to be
accepted, acknowledged and responded to.

But there's another problem to face. Often,
we feel that if we've effectively pushed our emotions into some kind of submission, we've dealt
with everything. Conquering feelings of pain or
denying the reality of the depth of mourning
through stoical denial of genuine human emotions can leave us emotionally desolate—or worse.
And anger left undealt with can quickly turn into
bitterness. Furthermore, people are often bewil-
dered by completely false ideas and speak of God

having "taken the child from them." How often it is suggested that God "took back" the life He had earlier "given from heaven." But this unscriptural idea is no more true for having been so frequently parroted or so poetically spoken at the funerals of young children. However well-intended, such misguided words both miss the mark of truth and build walls of fear. You may say, "If God took my child, how can I trust Him with my own life? Why should I trust a God who cares so little for my deepest, most fragile needs and emotions?" But listen, loved ones: God didn't and doesn't "take babies because He needs them in heaven."

So allow understanding to enter your soul. If you recognize anger over the loss of your child, deal with it now. The capacity of the human mind to go down its dead-end labyrinthine ways is amazing. We may think that suppression will help us overcome the pain, but it never does. Grief often includes submerged feelings of either fear or anger. These feelings *can* be dealt with, and here's how.

A major dynamic in the process of working through one's grief is found in the simple act of talking—to God, to family and to friends in your support system.

We need to talk to each other. One of the greatest lies our soul's enemy conjures is that what concerns you isn't worth anybody else's time. (Or that the only place you can turn is to someone that you pay to listen—a psychiatrist, doctor or pastor.) While these professionals may be very helpful and certainly have their place, be sure to allow your family, friends and church fellowship to help you work through the hard times related to your loss.

Begin with prayer. I mean, just talk to God. Talk with the Lord about the child you once had. Openly describe your bewilderment, and ask your questions. Believe in His love's willingness to embrace you in your pain—and even to understand your fears. But, dear friend, don't *blame* Him. Trust Him.

Further, if you feel the desire to do so, express your love toward your child. Do it before God. While we know that communicating with a loved one is *not* possible (and attempting to do so opens a person to being deceived by Satan), we *can* talk freely with God about all our feelings, asking any questions our hearts want to ask. But remember, if you have felt any anger toward God, let these truths we've covered bring a change of mind. He knows our hearts and not only forgives our misunderstandings, but also as the one perfect, loving Father, He welcomes our coming to Him—even spilling out our tears, our sorrow and our heartache. Bring it all into His presence. He not only will accept your heart cry, but *He will also comfort you.*

Let any heartbreak open the doors to discovering God's infinite mercy, His gentleness and His graciousness. He's the redeemer, and His loving kindness and mercy are past finding out. I encourage you to talk with Abba—that's the Hebrew word for "Daddy." His Holy Spirit wants to help you do that—and He's the best comforter of all.[2]

Remember, too, that God promises a reunion someday with your child. *Meaning* comes to the miscarrying mother: "I may not have been able to receive my child now, but my pregnancy was not a waste of time." *Hope* comes to the parents of a stillborn child or a child who died early in infancy: "We never got a chance to know you, but we shall, someday." And for the mother who chose an abortion, there is *peace*. "One day we will meet again in heaven, where our relationship will be whole and restored." In the light of the meaning, hope and peace God gives, it is perfectly proper to say, "I'll hold you in heaven." There will be a day of meeting your child.

In 1 Thessalonians 4, the apostle Paul examined the implications of the coming of Christ, helping people understand how the dead will be resurrected at Jesus' coming. He helped them understand how the living and the dead, who are prepared through a relationship with God, will be gathered together in one grand and mighty reunion. It was in this context that he told them, "Comfort one another with these words. We shall always be with the Lord."[3] When we are eternally gathered unto the living God, who made us, we shall be with Him forever —*and* with one another. It's not a dream, a myth or a humanly concocted fable. Our real and resurrected Savior, Jesus Christ, has promised this to all who trust in Him, and we can count on it. He's the fullness of Truth—the Son of God!

PUT GUILT IN ITS PLACE

I'm convinced that guilt is a natural part of the grief cycle. It's the human response of trying to find a logical, explainable answer for every tragedy.

Yet the ramifications of unresolved guilt are profound, resulting in

- shaken assurance, as we begin to doubt the very foundations upon which our life is built;
- crippled confidence, as we move through each day with foggy uncertainty, often unable to deal with the demands those days bring; and
- fragile faith, as we begin to wonder if or how God fits into life's harsh realities.

But God has a remedy for all these symptoms that guilt produces. He calls us to *confront* guilt—to put it in its place. He doesn't require this for the purpose of reopening a wound but, rather, for the purpose of allowing us to deal conclusively with any condemnation or doubt we may feel so that we might find freedom from it. You see, when our emotions are vulnerable, the adversary—Satan—preys on our pain, clawing those raw emotions with guilt or condemnation. Particularly in the wake of a death, feelings of unfounded guilt may abound.

For example, I remember how my own son-in-law was racked by guilt over the death of his brother in a tragic accident, because he had missed praying for him that day. Listen, loved one: Rest your guilt-driven grief on God's grace. Please, in Jesus' name, lay aside those feelings of guilt.

> *Rest your guilt-driven grief on God's grace.*

Sometimes, however, a portion of the guilt is founded. I can't deny the existence—and necessity—of the healthy dynamic of this guilt, for I have met too many who, through it, found relief. Some, stricken with the remorse and grief over their decision to have an abortion, have been right to acknowledge their failure and even *more* righteous to bring it humbly to our loving, forgiving Father God. If this is the case with your heart, it's important to let the guilt do its job, bringing you to repentance. Cleansing and full forgiveness will follow, for there is no decision or choice we could have made that's powerful enough to keep us from the cleansing, healing power of God's grace in Jesus Christ.

Come to Him.

Once your relationship with God is restored, your guilt has served its purpose and no longer has any place in your life. Let it go. And refuse its argument to regain any place in tormenting your mind or your feelings.

Being rid of guilt—either imagined or real guilt that has been resolved through the blood of Jesus Christ—is, however, sometimes easier described than done. But listen! God Himself has provided the means by which we can launch and sustain a victory over guilt. By the prophet Isaiah, God commanded, "Sing and shout because of what I've done. I have redeemed, I have blotted out, so sing and shout."[4] God's Word says it simply: Sing. Why not do it *now*. Quietly, as you sit where you are—at least hum the tune:

> Amazing grace, how sweet the sound,
> That saved a wretch like me.
> I once was lost but now am found;
> Was blind and now I see.[5]

When you begin to sing, praise God thankfully rather than trying to reason everything out. His Holy Spirit will begin loosening any chains that seem to bind you to feelings of guilt.

And if the archliar persists in plaguing you with any further condemnation, simply rest your case on the presence of God's living Word:

> So there is now no condemnation awaiting those who belong to Christ Jesus. For the power of the life-giving Spirit—and this power is mine through Christ Jesus—has freed me from the vicious circle of sin and death.[6]

Notes

1. Romans 8:28.
2. See John 14:15-18 and Galatians 4:6.
3. 1 Thessalonians 4:18,17.
4. See Isaiah 44:22-23.
5. John Newton, "Amazing Grace." Public domain.
6. Romans 8:1-2, *TLB*.

CHAPTER 7

THE HEARTBEAT
OF LOVE

This is My body which is broken for you.

1 CORINTHIANS 11:24

As we find practical steps to take through our studying the truth of God's Word, let's proceed to another level of need. What can we do to help stanch the flow of lost lives and lost hope resulting from abortion?

There are attitudes to be assessed and actions to take, and the heartbeat of both is in one word: *Love.* Love that reaches with life to cast out fear.

A great many people today have deep feelings about abortion—feelings that tug, anger, pinch and strangle. But I wish everyone who has ever been concerned about or scarred by abortion could have been at one particular morning worship service. What happened, right in the middle of a worship service with several thousand people present, would, I think, affect anyone's thinking. That morning everyone felt good about *not* having abortions—but no one felt smug, self-righteous or superior for having this feeling.

Here's the story.

I'll call her Tammy, to protect her real identity. She wasn't a girl without sexual values, but neither did her life have a spiritual base. Some months into her new-city experience and her new job, Tammy met a nice fellow. They began to date and, not because they were generally promiscuous, but because they were simply human and because neither had any personal spiritual experience, strength or guidance, Tammy and her boyfriend had intercourse—and Tammy got pregnant.

He ran.

Yep, her boyfriend was scared.

That might not be a very noble response on his part, but before you go too hard on the boy, remember what we're talking about. Two people in their early twenties, hardly even adults in some respects, without spiritual roots, carried away by emotion. Well, this fellow was anything but ready for a family, so he ran.

But Tammy couldn't run.

The problem was inside her body. And the small mass of cells multiplying at a phenomenal rate every day brought terrifying fear to the girl.

She was new to the city, new to her work environment and newly in love—at least she had thought so. And now she was about to become a new parent—and without a partner.

Tammy wrestled with the plaguing fears. She called her parents and they immediately and completely rejected her, offering nothing of support, guidance or counsel except, "Don't come home." It was then she decided to check the

Yellow Pages for some place at which she might inquire about an abortion.

The previous edition of the Yellow Pages was much the same as in most cities of our nation. Dozens of abortion clinics were listed—veiled with names that suggest counsel and consultation but which usually advise "Abort." Occasionally, an alternative point of counsel is available (in this book there was one). But even then, it was not from a Christian perspective—that is, not with the patient wisdom and gentle power in the touch the Spirit of God brings to any human need.

However, a *new* phone book had just been published—and for the first time in more than a dozen years since the Supreme Court's infamous *Roe v. Wade* decision, which brought on the wholesale practice of abortion in the United States, this phone book had a number to call that offered something different. There was an ad with a picture of one hand reaching for another, with the words "Touchpoint—Free Pregnancy Testing . . . Immediate Results—Referrals offered."

Tammy called.

What Tammy didn't know is that the number she called reached a phone in an office opened only days before, opened because one church caught a vision and thousands of its members believed in it enough to give the funds needed to launch its fulfillment.

The vision was

- to provide a point of reference for pregnancy counseling without imposing a spiritual demand on the inquirer but distinctly discouraging abortion—and providing options;
- to trust the holy to bless the counselees by causing their hearts to open to the gentle understanding shown; and
- that by this process, lives would be touched, women ministered to and babies saved.

And Tammy had called—which leads back to the worship service I mentioned taking place that special morning, the special day that Tammy came to church with her baby.

You see, following that phone call, a lot of time, a lot of patience and a gracious, unpressuring influence had been shown and given to Tammy. She immediately recognized a quality of life—of love—she'd never known before. The result was that Tammy decided against abortion; a little while later, she received Jesus Christ as her Savior, and on this special Sunday had brought her newborn baby girl for dedication to the Lord.

Although there was no baby's daddy or husband present beside Tammy, elders from this congregation stood with their wives beside the young woman.

*Because you prayed,
you gave and you loved,
here in my arms is wholeness,
not brokenness.*

Preparing to take Communion, everyone in the room held in hand the broken bread, over which Jesus spoke saying, "This is My body which is broken for you."[1] The pastor spoke about the intent of Christ—that through His brokenness, a wholeness be ministered to mankind—and, at that point, invited Tammy and the baby to come to the platform.

The worshipers, though not used to such an interruption at the Lord's Table, listened with tear-moistened eyes as Tammy's story was related. Then the pastor took the baby in his arms and said, "This is as dramatic a case as I think you'll ever see, in which brokenness is made whole through the love of Jesus. This baby would have been broken in the womb, but she wasn't. Because you prayed, you gave and you loved, Tammy found new possibilities; and here in my arms is wholeness, not brokenness."

It was an incredible morning, and all the more wonderful when, shortly after that service, a phone call to Tammy's parents found a changed attitude on their part. Their hearts had been touched that someone, somewhere had helped their daughter in her personal crisis. Now they wanted to do their part.

Today, Tammy is home, having been lovingly welcomed there by her folks, who are helping their daughter move forward in life—with their little granddaughter as well.

You'll pardon me if I seem to relate this in a slightly emotional way, because I was there.

I was the pastor.

Ours was the congregation.

I held that baby in my arms and presented it before Father God in the rite of dedication. But the reason I was moved was not simply because a baby's life was spared; it was because the event itself would never have happened had not something else occurred.

It involved three very large steps in a change of attitude. In relating them to you in the next chapter, I risk being badly misunderstood, but I've decided to run that risk. Too many lives are at stake for smallness on my part to prompt hesitation or, for that matter, smallness on any of our part. I think there is a smallness in many of us, not produced by a willful stinginess of soul but by the fear to love.

Let me describe my starting place, where those three steps brought me and those who walked that path with me. They brought us, in the end, to a larger place of service and a greater ministering of Jesus' love.

Note

1. 1 Corinthians 11:24.

CHAPTER 8

THREE STEPS TO LOVING

God demonstrates His own love toward us, in that wh
were still sinners, Christ died for us.

ROMANS 5:8

RESPONDING EMOTIONALLY: OVERCOMING SELF-RIGHTEOUSNESS

In one way or another all of us are people walking through a living graveyard.

Everywhere we go, among everyone we meet every day, there are the walking dead. They are people so radically impacted by death in one way or another that they are candidates not only for *healing* but also for resurrection. Death has come to them in one or more of a hundred forms. There isn't anyone you'll meet today that hasn't been touched by

- the death of relationships,
- the death of dreams,
- the death of a business enterprise,
- the death of a loved one.

These aren't negative observations made by one who views life dismally. I'm simply noting the fact that death is present in many, many ways. And you and I have been prepared to bring a living answer!

But before that can happen, many of us need a melting of our hearts. I know I did—and a number of factors contributed to God's bringing it about. It began with an ulterior viewpoint of a self-righteousness I didn't see in my own attitude.

I knew the Word of God and I knew abortion was wrong: I opposed it, prayed for people who practiced it and prayed against its spread in our nation. And I sometimes went mad when I saw television news reports displaying the militant actions of so called pro-choice advocates. But as I said earlier, God radically changed my attitude without changing my convictions.

For example, I had never had to deal with the victim of forcible incest or rape—a woman pregnant with a baby produced by an involuntary or violent act. Nor had I ever thought much about the agony of soul in a woman whose child within was known to be deformed. Nor had I considered the emotional plight of the husband whose wife's health was imperiled to the point that she would probably bear the child at the expense of her own life.

Rape.

Incest.

Known deformity in the womb.

Mother's health.

These were issues I had hardly considered. For my part, I was not ready to concede that abortion was the answer to any of these situations. And I must gently say that I'm still not. But at the same time, I have had to come to the point that I not only can but simply must also allow for the price of *fear*—yes, even *selfishness* if anyone may judge it to be so—when someone chooses an abortion in any of these situations.

Listen.

Listen, please. I make such allowance, not because I believe it may necessarily be the right choice, but because all of us, as fallible human beings, have all made wrong choices! When I see someone who has made a wrong choice—even in the face of alternative counseling that I have given—I cannot, in the Spirit of Christ, sit in judgment of them for that.

As a fallible, sinning human being, I, too, have felt fear that has begotten actions less than worthy or faith filled. And now, suddenly, I was being shaken by God's Word at the very point at which my self-righteousness toward abortion had been so conveniently sustained. I was being confronted by the Holy Spirit, being reminded that I was to love exactly as He loves.

> But God demonstrates His own love toward us, in that while we were still sinners, Christ died for us.[1]

Of course, I knew that verse before, but I had always applied it to the doctrine of God's salvation, not to the duty of a Christian. In other words, I could see how necessary it was that God loved me first, in order to reach me with His love.

His love is unbounded, unending and fully offered in advance.

Beyond my blindness to His way, my ignorance of His will, my indifference to His Spirit, and in spite of my self-serving sinfulness, His love was unconditional. His Word is marvelously clear and the truth incredibly freeing: His love is unbounded, unending and fully offered *in advance.*

But I'd never had it settle upon my soul that He was calling me to love people the same way He does. My evangelical orthodoxy required me to insist that I had to overcome sin by resisting it in others—not only in myself. Wherever I found it, I found myself succumbing to a watchdog mentality of critiquing my culture rather than a shepherd mind-set toward lovingly seeking the lost. That is, until I thought through the way Jesus overcame sin. The way He overcame sin was in surrendering Himself to love—to stand forgivingly before sin until His love overcame it.

Now I was being forced to confront this fact: God wanted me to love people who had abortions, whether or not I agreed with their action. And He wanted me to do it without the usual verbal appendage, "Okay, I'll love them, but I still hate their sin."

I think we may too easily employ that ruse to satisfy our emotional outrage, and when we do, the hatred too often spills over and poisons our best efforts at serving the lost. Can you imagine Jesus on the cross saying, "Father, forgive them, they don't know what they're doing . . . and I hate it. I can't say how *much* I hate it, but I'll still love them, though I assure you I hate their sin"?

Oh, don't make any mistake. Don't think I'm soft on sin or that I am arguing that God is.

Never.

The reason Christ *died* for sin is that sin is deadly serious business, and the death price has to be paid in full, one way or the other. When we take matters into our own hands, death prevails. But when we trust what His almighty power has accomplished in *His* dying, life can win!

I was beginning to realize that my unloving attitude was not a necessary ingredient to ensure a sufficient payment for people's sins. God didn't need me to be mad at their sin—to hate it—in order to assure it was fully compensated for. He had only commissioned me to be a reconciler—to help people be reconciled to Him by reaching them with His love, understanding and tenderness.[2] When I came to terms with the fact that a lot of people aborting children were no less or no more sinful than I was, I found I was far more ready to understand the fears, emotion and torment of a woman facing a pregnancy she feared or didn't want. I *wasn't* any more ready to agree she should terminate it, but I *was* more ready to accept the person who made that decision.

RESPONDING INTELLECTUALLY: SURVEYING THE POTENTIAL FOR DISASTER

I was now ready to do something about it. And something does need to be done.

The painful matter of abortion cannot interminably go on being condemned by the indignant while it is promoted by its proponents. The issue isn't only that life's possibilities are being removed from the millions affected; it has to do with attitudes toward the *control* of life. Life as it concerns *all of us*—the billions on this planet right now.

Thoughtful analysis of the moral question concerning abortion and those who propose that on-demand privilege be outlawed are not simplistically pontificating a pro-life cause. They are forcing us to look at the drift set in motion once a society accepts the privilege of terminating *any* human life at will *and* with impunity.

Where does the process stop?

If life is disallowed in the womb on the front end of its span, what is to stop the evolution of a social policy that may at will, anytime and with impunity, stop it on the other end? If we can legally take a baby's life in the womb, will the next step be taking Grandpa's life when he's old—exterminating him as a willful act simply because he's more an inconvenience than a contribution to the community? ("After all, he isn't doing well anyway.")

And then euthanasia. Mercy killing, they call it.

When suffering intensifies and the agony of the family looking on is only exceeded by the agony of a loved one in the throes of death as violent disease and indescribable torturous pain rack an aging body, what then?

Who should play God?

That question probes our social consciousness, and people who think abortion is but a single issue need to look into the extended ramifications of its acceptance.

Further, this doesn't even begin to explore the implications of genetic engineering and alternative approaches to conception and childbearing. Who can forecast the long-range effects of present research and activity in genetic manipulation, recombinant DNA, extra-uterine conception, surrogate motherhood, sperm banks and the moral and humane issues raised by cloning?

I'm not ready to prophesy the birth of a troop of Frankenstein monsters, but neither can I retire to an ostrichlike stance of passivity, pretending that present trends are only passing fads. Man is dabbling in the *control* of life, not merely its reproduction, and there is no scriptural indication that his God-given assignment to "subdue" the earth and "replenish it" even includes much of what he's into right now.

I'm certainly not resistant to the scientific research that has often blessed mankind with benevolent results. But I don't think we can neglect the fact that there are some very negative implications in some of what is happening. Social ethics are spiritual issues, and they are being dramatically impacted by today's applied biological research.

RESPONDING SPIRITUALLY: GETTING INVOLVED

I recently appealed to our congregation to do something to indicate our interest in the life of the unborn child. I wasn't proposing a march on city hall; I didn't offer placards or design a sit-in at a clinic. I certainly *did* make clear my revulsion at the hideous actions of people who bomb clinics in that insane expression of protest. But I further said, "We can't do *nothing*."

Following that Sunday, I received a letter from a man who I think expresses what some Christians suppose to be a spiritual response: "I don't think the Church should be involved in political issues," he wrote.

I could hardly believe my eyes: A *political issue?!*

We were talking about LIFE.

We were talking about morality.

We were talking about loving people who are afraid to accept the life conceived within them, and trying to lovingly serve them amid those fears.

However well-intended or supposedly spiritual his motivation, this man reflected the fact that in all of us there is the temptation to find some escape from responsibility for action. I know I would rather leave it all alone; the subject bothers me. But I had to listen to Proverbs 31:8-9:

> Open your mouth for the speechless, in
> the cause of all who are appointed to die.
> Open your mouth, judge righteously, and
> plead the cause of the poor and needy.

I had (1) faced the facts of my self-righteousness, (2) broadened my perspective on what was happening in some people facing tough situations and (3) now taken a hard look at social and moral questions facing us today. But with the third step, what could I do?

Well, I'm not a very political, protest-type person. In fact, I have difficulty with the idea of the Church marching in any arena other than on its knees. I'm sure my feelings wouldn't seem tough enough to satisfy a lot of good Christians, while others would doubtless assess my position as being too strict.

But I did arrive at a point of action that somehow strikes me as one balanced between judgment and mercy. It involves

- ministering *personally* in the spirit and the truth I've presented in this book; and
- ministering *publicly* by serving people in our society with a living option, through providing the type of resource that resulted in the rescue of Tammy's baby.

The addendum that follows may be utilized as you or any church leader you have contact with may wish to pursue. For me it accomplished the third step in *loving*. I hope it might help you do the same.

There *is* a turnaround taking place in the thoughts and actions of many today. I know, because of a massive surge of God's grace that

helped me turn—to rethink the problems of just one arena of pain tormenting people like you and me.

I hope this chronicle of my journey, self-discovery and ensuing truth-discoveries in God's Word make a full circle possible. May you know Christ's healing and fullness, and may you become a transmitter of His life.

With a heart full of His love and forgiveness, let us each be quick to obey and constant in doing what the angel commended long ago: *"Go . . . and speak to the people all the words of this life."*[3]

Notes

1. Romans 5:8.
2. See 2 Corinthians 5:18-21.
3. Acts 5:20.

Addendum

I deeply believe everyone who has chosen to place God's value on human life, especially life in the womb, should be involved in some practical ways of supporting those agencies that plead this cause and that offer open doors to women who come for aide when pregnant.

Billy Graham modeled this order of care and concern when, in 1975, he opened his home to a group of believers who met to form the Christian Action Council—the result being the formation of a network of Crisis Pregnancy Centers. The location called Touchpoint, mentioned in Tammy's story earlier in this book, was one such center, although in various communities different names are used since these service centers are locally founded and supported.

The most commonly referenced network today is CareNet, and information on one in your area may be found at their website www.care-net.org, where a means of follow-through is clearly set in place

- for a woman or family, couple or individual facing the challenge of an unexpected pregnancy;
- for a church or other group to explore ways they might provide support or volunteer aide to serve this ministry in their area;
- for people like you and me to contribute financial support to this highly important and redemptive service to our communities.

Anna and I make periodic financial contributions to CareNet-type enterprises and strongly encourage everyone to do the same. Further, I have often spoken at local and regional fund-raisers for such ministries as well; I am happy to donate my services and steward whatever influence God has given me both to encourage those *dedicated* people who reach with His love in this way and to motivate those *sensitive* people who will fund such life-saving, healing outreaches.

(I was hesitant to mention my habit of speaking in such venues when I have been able, because my work and travel schedule rarely allows it. My purpose is not to prompt invitations, which I so often cannot accept, but to urge other recognized pastors, speakers and leaders to model the same availability.)

Dear Jack,

I have read *I'll Hold You in Heaven* and, while doing so, came to the time and place where I have made my decision to receive the Lord Jesus Christ as my personal Savior.

I would appreciate it if you would send me the gift copy of *NEWBORN: Your New Life with Christ* as I begin life with Him.

Please mail to:

Your Name _____ Address _____

City _____ State _____ Zip _____

NEWBORN: Your New Life with Christ will be sent to you free of charge.

Mail this request to:
Dr. Jack W. Hayford
The King's College and Seminary
14800 Sherman Way
Van Nuys, CA 91405